An American Gallery

By John Calvin Rezmerski

Held for Questioning
An American Gallery

An American Gallery

poems by

John Calvin Rezmerski

Three Rivers Press
Pittsburgh 1977

PS
3568
.E95
.A7

for P.J., Bill, and Caroline

Acknowledgments

Acknowledgment is gratefully made to editors of the following
magazines and anthologies in which some of these poems first
appeared.

Blue Cloud Quarterly: "Sioux Indian Museum, Rapid City."
Crazy Horse: "In a Restaurant in Minnesota."
Dacotah Territory: "A Dream of Indians."
Etc.: "Grandfather."
Heartland II: "Some Good Things Left After the War with the Sioux."
Jam To-day: "Miracle," and "Dr. Williamson Instructs the Artist Concerning
His Representations of the Sioux."
Mennonite Life: "For Martin Luther King, Jr."
1972 Minnesota Poetry Anthology: "Each at Its Own Time."
25 Minnesota Poets: "Driving at Night."
Moons and Lion Tailes: "Watching Leech Lake from a High Bank."
New: American and Canadian Poetry: "The Land."
New Salt Creek Reader: "Advertisement."
Northeast: "The Baptism of Annie Johnson," and "Economy."
Poetry Now: "Superhighway."
Sumac: "Poem for the Mothers of New York."
The Lamp in the Spine: "Why Henry Thoreau Never Married."
Three Rivers Poetry Journal: "Pigeons," "Male Chauvinist Roadside Pig," and
"Prodigal Son."

The publication of this book is supported by a grant from
the National Endowment for the Arts in Washington, D.C.,
a Federal agency.

The publisher wishes to thank Michael Kaniecki and Sarah Verbits for help in
the production of this book.

Library of Congress Catalog Card Number: 76-55071
ISBN 0-915606-02-X
Copyright © 1977 by Three Rivers Press
Printed and bound in the United States of America

Book design by Gerald Costanzo

CONTENTS

I. WHY HENRY THOREAU NEVER MARRIED

II. ALONG THE ROAD ON FOOT

07777

III. EACH AT ITS OWN TIME

IV. SOME GOOD THINGS LEFT AFTER THE WAR WITH THE SIOUX

I. WHY HENRY THOREAU NEVER MARRIED

AN AMERICAN GALLERY

"I wish there was a gallery
around here I could visit,"
he said.
                She said,
"You mean an art gallery
or a shooting gallery?"

That's where he was quiet,
so she answered herself:
"The peanut gallery, I guess."

"Everything," he said.

THE LAND

The land is not beaten yet.
Plenty of places you can see
prairie fighting back
corn and wheat,
woods fighting back
at parks and pastures.
Trees keep coming back green
out of last year's cut brush.
Some places the land
just won't give up,
putting its rocks out front
like gritted teeth.
Trying to beat the land
is like trying to beat
sense into your mother.
The only way to win
is to kill her.

POEM FOR THE MOTHERS OF NEW YORK

This city is full of pregnant women
following their bellies
to the grocery stores,
the benches by the park grass,
the stairways over antique shops.
A hundred thousand
heavy former virgins
waddle to their beds
full of pistachio ice cream
and the hands of their lovers.
Traffic lights change just for them,
and drugstores open late on Sundays.

They clean the streets as they walk,
they breathe out fresh air.
Among the horns and brakes
and dented fenders
someone loves them,
maybe even a truck driver
loves their slow way
of crossing.

THE BAPTISM OF ANNIE JOHNSON

1. Among a clump of humid Christians
in a yard on Seventh Street,
she and grandfather
have sense enough to sleep.
It's a good day to be saved,
dressed in bleached cotton,
white and wrinkled in her basket
like a chestnut in its husk.

She has been washed and exposed to strangers
while a radio sings hymns to industry.
She will hear the different ways
of holding a pencil,
and which one is right.
Here is the visible church.

2. She has faith in milk,
but mother is among the guests.
Older children are next door
swiping apples
to throw at each other.
She wants to know
forgiveness
but grandmother
steals all of God's attention
with a gouty foot.
Clouds pile up in the West,

lightning tickles the horizon.
She begins to cry;
sin or no sin, she's hungry.

3. Her thunderstorm is ready.
Water hits her harder now.
We file into the house,
bearing ham and potato salad and cake
and children
as though boarding the ark.
She cries as though
afraid for her life.

ACCOUNT

As a child learning guilt,
I used to play a game called Martyr,
put stones in my shoes,
gave my allowance to the Church, and
let my dinner get cold
so it wouldn't taste so good.
Even played stupid, mouth shut
when I knew someone was wrong.
I used to hear a cavernous voice
yelling up encouragement from my bowels:
"You brought it on yourself," or
"No aspirin, no aspirin, no aspirin."
I knew about justice.
I grew up without hate,
amazed at loving nobody,
with a curious fondness
for cold meat and lukewarm coffee.

THE MODERN PURITAN SPEAKS

I know how much less than me
everyone else does and knows,
but to be fair,
perhaps it's not their fault.
They were not given my tenacity.
Even when I had hemorrhoids
I had them better
than anyone else.
Perfection is the only goal
worth a serious man's trouble.
I have spent years
polishing my delivery
(only the lazy speak poorly)
memorizing vocabulary
and quotations from Emerson,
writing them on a sleeve
I keep in my mind.
There is no sense saying something
unless you make it sound
authoritative.
I am the Lord's rhetorician,
the tonguelash of righteousness:
I uphold ideals
that are down-to-earth.
I stand strong on solid ground
where the ancients are laid
speaking of their superiority
to this generation of self-abusers.
I, too, am
better than the living.

WHY HENRY THOREAU NEVER MARRIED

Something about a woman
is green and secret
like a pod of beans.
So I began by studying
beans,
folding back the shells
looking for seeds,
splitting open each seed
looking for the soul of the bean,
looking for some reason to say
women are holy.
I thought to start
I could pick them over,
plant them, harvest them,
go out in the field and sit with them,
cut away the clutching weeds around them,
handle them, finger them,
take them to my house,
talk to them,
taste them, sort out
the sweet and the starchy.
I could give each one a separate name,

I could know all their secrets.
Cell by cell,
I could know them all.

Three days of rain and ninety or above. This afternoon the clouds lie right on the lake. The water is thick and gray as mercury. Fifty yards out, a colorless goose drifts, stabbing the water as though to rip a hole in it. Must be just a big duck. But its whole head goes down the hole. Watching, I imagine the cold water on my eyes, and close them.

Gone. I glance around to see where it's flown. Maybe some huge fish got it! Too long to be down for food. But there, without a splash, closer, facing me, a flash of white breast and greenish head. A loon! I've never seen one before! Maybe this is the one whose melancholy giggle kept me up last night.

It curls under down through the hold in the water. I count seconds up to sixty-three, and there it is again — the loon, silent and sudden as though the special creation has happened again just to fill up this empty afternoon.

An hour before sunset, the sun makes a bright road across the water to the far shore. A quarter mile out, loons start calling. I count eight — no, nine! No, eleven! I can't keep track. They dive and rise one by one, one by two. Maybe fifteen. Today I saw thousands of minnows close as my fingers. I know what the fish have been doing, and it's a fat year for loons, gliding down to feast under the slippery water, each time coming up farther out toward the middle of the bay.

Thirty feet from them, half a dozen loud boats pass, two with noses up, showing off musclebound motors. The waves make the loons bob like hunters' decoys, but they keep on feeding. This is loon property.

A plane comes over, low. Its pontoons sag, its engines growl like earth-giants fighting to throw each other to the moon. Ggggrrrraaaaauuuuugggghhhh! The loons spook, straight for shore without a sound, low over the water, wings beating high. All but one, who waits. And struts fifty feet above the lake on a curving course toward shore, as if to show the plane how easy it can be, even on a full belly.

LET ME NOT FOR THE MARRIAGE OF TWO DOGS ADMIT IMPERMANENCE

It is a damp spring day, the grass still not green. The sun is doing its best. The robins are setting up housekeeping, the grackles have gathered to harass squirrels. People have not yet started going for walks in the woods. I stay around the house.

Two dogs arrive. They seem to know each other. She is bigger, black and brown, a beautiful face like a German shepherd, but half the size. He is little, wiry, red-yellow, some kind of terrier. They nuzzle a little, and he boldly works along her flank, all the way back. Then he is behind her. She is so tall, but she smells so right. She dances a few steps away, as if to say not now, but he insists and soon his elbows rest on her back, and he pumps his hips, wearing a doggy smile, faster and faster, eager, not out of breath. She is patient with him.

Then it's over. He runs around her twice — Was it good for you, too, was it good, huh? She stretches all her legs at once, more like a cat than a dog. She doesn't need to say it. She goes to a little spruce tree and pisses on it. He comes back to her, sniffs her face, sniffs between her legs, and pisses on the same tree. He is not obliged to support her, she doesn't have to clean up after him. They are not bound to each other by any document, but together they have had a joyful moment, together they have claimed a tree.

ECONOMY

Love will dry out your brains —
but I digress —
the best magic comes from the glands, anyway.
It is recorded of the Americans
that they worshipped the spirit of the hammer,
that the only music they had
was the crumpling together
of flesh and steel.
They were people
who loved to watch dancing,
working men who sang
jingles that proved
they were not afraid of money.

But they were first-class jugglers.

The women called birth a small death,
thought witchcraft a business
of turning flesh into gold.
The men ran shouting over the land
looking for amulets.
They ate wristwatches —
but I digress —
the child should not hold the father's spear.

PIGEONS

The pigeons leave droppings
on upstairs windows
even as they are being cleaned.
Grandma asks Grandpa
"Why do you keep those pigeons?
Why don't you get rid of them?
They're no good for
anything."
          "Listen,"
          he says,
"When I'm sick
they moan and groan for me."

PRODIGAL SON

Unable to be the son of anyone forever,
I went out of my father's mind,
leaving his law behind me
like a heretic done believing in Hell.

I was prepared to be wicked,
to walk the mad road over the mountains,
breathe the breath of foreign women,
gorge myself on the sweet pork
that can only be bought with knives
or stolen information.
I was free to do my worst.

And breathed the smells
of a pimpled girl from Philadelphia,
slept on a hide-a-bed,
became a connoisseur of submarine sandwiches
bought with a pushbroom and footnotes.
That was the worst I was able to do.

WHITE BLUES SINGER

The wormy-looking blonde
with the big nose
had a bellyful of people —
stood ready to swallow the microphone
singing
until she was singing so hot
her face melted.
She began to glow.
Right in front of us —
turned into a moth,
a flicker of dusty wings.

MIRACLE

A man who had gone through
a silage chopper almost up to his shoulder
told me he had not enjoyed it
exactly,
but he did remember being happy
at coming so close to salvation.
It was Sunday
and he had been repentant.
He had not seen God
exactly,
but he had heard him,
and picked up just one eternal verity
before his damnfool uncle
switched off the machine.
The sound of the shredding arm, he said,
was shaped by God, and
came in clear syllables,
saying,
take it easy, damn you, take your time.

GREAT-GRANDFATHER

At seventy-seven years
he should not have been pumping that water,
with his heart.
The blood went right to his head,
my Grandmother says,
he turned blue and fell over
and died right by the drain
just to prove to his neighbors
every time it rained
the water came up red
as blood in the pump.

EASTER: A TRUE REPORT

The priest at Easter Mass
says: "Let us pray
for the repose of the soul
of"
he mentions a name
"who died and was buried . . ."
I expect him to say
"And rose again on the third day"
but he corrects himself, saying
"And will be buried tomorrow."

EVERY MAN HIS FAIR SHARE

After you can't see
the ugly flowers people send
when you are no longer sick,
they shave you and trim your nails,
buttonhook your mouth closed
so you will not offend,
and give you your first ride
in a long black Cadillac.

MALE CHAUVINIST ROADSIDE PIG

The cars go by
with girls.
Girls.
And I think.
Please stop.
Please stop.
Come on,
please stop.
In my mind I am
a traffic cop,
father figure
in blue and whistle,
and I flag down
their fine autobodies,
and award them
certificates
for fine driving.
And when they
glide away,
I wave.
And when cars go by
with men driving,
I wave:
move along,
keep it moving.

II. ALONG THE ROAD ON FOOT

SUPERHIGHWAY

Interstate 80
crosscountry
at sixty or seventy
the road is strewn
with woodchucks
crushed
skunks squeezed into one last spray
possums sleeping in blood
foxes gone to dark red
deer here and there
sometimes
a porcupine or rabbit
or a scattered bird
you can't tell what kind at this speed
and once in a while
the busted body of a person
someone who dared
step far enough into the past
to set out along the road on foot.

IN A RESTAURANT IN MINNESOTA

A man who works on the railroad
tells me about the couplings
of excited yard engines.
His voice throbs like a diesel idling.
He tells me what happens
on sidings at night
when unlighted coaches roll through.
I buy him a second cup of coffee
because he believes in God
and his secrets make his hands shake.
He tells me his wife knits afghans
while he dirties himself
mating boxcars.
His wife is Swedish and German,
he does not know what he is,
except Republican.

DRIVING AT NIGHT

The radio brings whole cities
into my head.
Philadelphia, Kansas City,
Houston.
Louisville.
St. Louis, Minneapolis.
They fly in at me
out of the dark
full of people talking, dying,
committing crimes.
They are at war,
blasting each other with static,
pushing each other aside
in the air
as though my head
is the last safe place
for a city to be.

ADVERTISEMENT

I want to be like
the people in television commercials,
I want to have no problems
industry can't solve in a minute.
I want to eat and drink and bathe
myself into every home in America.
I want to be a public service message.
I want to go out to you
prepackaged
and at a great saving
and convenience.
I want to be easy to prepare.
I want to be instant.
I want to live between traumas and giggles,
sending you to the refrigerator.
Whether you believe me or not,
that's what I want.

CRIMINAL JUSTICE

I don't mean to say the rich have too much
power, but
once there was a man who
bludgeoned his wife and her lhasa apso
with a polo mallet
and bought himself the best trial you've ever seen,
getting off with temporary insanity
and several interviews on national TV.
Then he enjoyed himself, and got bored
and started reading books
and wound up deciding too much money
was dangerous
and made up his mind to give it all away.
He went out into the streets
just throwing money away,
a handful every block or so,
all over the city.
It wasn't till it was all gone
that they arrested him for aggravated littering
and hanged the only son of a bitch
who ever understood
why too much money is dangerous.

SEX AND VIOLENCE

Anywhere on this page
someone could love to
break in and kill me.
You could be in the middle of this
and be raped or slain
by an intruder.

We could make a deal —
which of us to be found naked,
which to be the assailant.

If you turn out to be more cruel,
I expect
to take at least as long
as an opera singer
who has just orgasmically intoned,
"Oh, I am murdered!
Oh, I die!"
and who goes on singing until
the end of the act,
the curtain falling modestly
to veil whatever comes next,
to cloak the afterlife
of that singer,
the fate of this writer,
the wishes of any
Jack the Ripper or
you, gentle reader,
with your tender skin.

A DREAM OF INDIANS

Paralyzed and posed
at a desk
in a museum case,
dressed in jeans,
white sport coat,
pink carnation,
T-shirt and paisley tie,
and on my head,
a bright orange hardhat.

People file past
in leather and feathers
admiring my costume,
my matched desk set,
wondering what
my dictionary is.
They point at my wall-clock,
saying:
How primitive!
and laugh because
my fly is open.

Here men with full hearts
teeter between now and then
face to face with the red energy,
the angular life
of a medicine man
wrapped in his blue blanket.
The picture of a perfect
reservation ranch
in the blue of winter,
housepaint on masonite,
proves again
the world is actually flat
with four corners.
And if it is round also,
there is no need to fight.
The sky is in its place
and the earth is as solid as ever.
Here the old elkskin clothes
are clean as freshmade,
and ready for ceremonies to begin.
Here a new life is made
and set out proud,
skill for sale,
but no souls are to be sold.

ON THE FRONTIER

An old cowboy in cracked chaps
buying a blue shirt
embroidered red and white.
Every day, his guns hang lower.
Every day, his horse gets fatter.
He pants after the schoolmarm
and marries the big woman with the bustle
who dances on the hotel stairs.
The shirt is for his wedding
which he has forgotten is over.
He is 200 years old and it's hard to remember
anything but how much he hates his mother.
He has worn his share of badges,
eaten his share of beef,
cut down his share of trees.
He looks out the window
and it is all his,
the whole countryside,
and not worth the time
with no Indians to protect it from.
When he is tired of laying in bed
and lonesome for enemies,
you or me (or anybody
who looks at a sunrise
instead of a sunset
he can ride into)
becomes an Indian to chase.
He mounts up,

fills his saddlebags,
visits the blacksmith,
the saloon,
the outhouse,
talks down to green kids
and herds them out
to save the railroad or the airport.
With portable sixguns,
portable radio,
portable lives.
When he goes out in his new shirt
it is a hundred years ago —
time to invent the fast draw.

Lecture hall half full, people here to hear this man speak for his people tonight. He says, "No going back to the blanket for modern Indians. BIA has been throwing a blanket over us for years."

I daydream of noble warriors with folded arms and eagle feathers.

He says, "You boyscouts and girlscouts think tents are so great — try it without your Coleman stove. You think Indians still live in tipis? I grew up in a two-room shack, holes in the roof and nothing to patch with. Wasn't a winter my front and back were both warm at the same time."

I picture my whole family telling side-by-side stories on a cold night around a campfire.

He says, "You probably wonder why I don't say Ugh. When I was little, things were so bad I said Ugh to everything. Now I'm tired of it, Kemo Sabe — ever wonder what that really means? It's what we used to call Custer."

We all laugh. But Custer is dead. Crazy Horse is dead. Little Crow is dead. Amos Huggins is dead. Raymond Yellow Thunder is dead.

Next the speaker from the government says, "Past misguided policies have disadvantaged the Indians. Now we must commit ourselves solidly to new programs, for feeding and housing and encouraging progress . . ."

And I am reminded how in a buffalo hunt, first you surround them.

DR. WILLIAMSON INSTRUCTS THE ARTIST
CONCERNING HIS REPRESENTATIONS OF THE SIOUX

I will paint them running,
they are like deer.

No, no, no, no,
the missionary tells the artist,
Don't compare them with animals.
They are like children.

Spoiled children, says the artist,
I will paint them shouting.

No, no, no, no,
They haven't had your chance,
they lack the means . . .

And the conscience, says the artist,
I will picture them with drawn knives.

No, no, no, no,
Even a savage knows righteousness and wickedness.

Especially wickedness, says the artist,

I will show them dancing wildly.

No, no, no, no,
In another generation
they will be as good as civilized.

When the sun is rising
we all claim to be westerners.

AT THE SLIDE SHOW

The Indian art slide show
narrator says
how amazing
primitives
took the time
and had the skill
to make things look
so evocative
of the modern.
A little Sioux girl
about three feet tall
gets up
and blocks the screen,
looking
straight down
the barrel of the projector.
And doesn't move
when her parents tell her to.

GRANDFATHER

At your anniversary Mass in July
the holy water was polluted
and nobody noticed.
Fewer of your friends came out this spring,
and Grandma wilts a little each summer
with the beans and the tomatoes.
The garden is played out,
even the worms don't go there so much.
The only thing that has stayed the same
is the smell of the sulfite smoke
and it no longer smells like money.
There is a stairway to your porch now,
and a hole between dining room and kitchen
to pass cups and dishes through.
I bet there is an old quart of peach brandy
in the cellar, and a tobacco can
hidden with some emergency money forgotten
while you waited in bed for your heart to quit.
It is your voice I remember best,
still half Polish,
and the roughness of your faded black sweater.
Remembering your whiskers on my cheeks
makes me feel like I'm six again.
The family never gets together
to play Pinochle any more.
The chicken house is empty,
even the dogs are gone

that stayed there when the last chicken was eaten.
It seems to me you used to keep pigeons.
Grandpa, if you had known my God
he would have protected you from yours.
He would have.
Your children are prospering
and you have dozens of great grandchildren.
Since you died we have acquired new one-way streets
and another stoplight.
And they're finally going to pave your street.
And according to the papers
Poland is still there.

III. EACH AT ITS OWN TIME

CLASSIFIED 1-A

You can look at me
in my current uniform
and not see scars
of the current war.
It's too bad you can't tell —
especially when the weather's so good —
how dangerous I am
in my silence about the dead,
my public ignorance
of classified information.
Look at me,
how my top-secret potential for bleeding,
my ignorance of camouflage,
invite target practice.
Look at me, I resemble
what's his name,
your brother-in-law,
who ruins the sunshine
and tightens your knuckles.
I know what you're thinking,
I should join the army
and let them
make something out of me.

PICTURES OF THE VIETNAM WAR DEAD

These are the men
the sergeants and officers
told to look alive.
Here they are all spread out
in Life magazine.
Life cannot deceive me,
I know the pictures were taken
after
these were corpses.
Some photographer
and some undertaker
and some cosmetician
molded them into smiles and frowns,
and snapped away.
I turn the page
several times
and find more faces.
I seem to have a year's subscription
to these faces,
different faces molded alike.

AFTER THE ATTACK

When they crawled out of the cellars
of the burned houses,
and came dirty and dripping
out of the sloughs
and saw how many of the dead were their children
and how bright the children's blood was
next to the dull adult blood,
and when they saw
how quickly flies light
and maggots are born
and saw
how hard it is to tell
human guts from a split hog's
and when they understood
how hated they were
they swallowed their tears
and puked
and saw the puke and tears
on the grass with the blood
and puked again.
And they wailed hoarse prayers
to let it not be real,
not be real children,
let them belong to somebody else,
let them be lambs,
let them be beasts,
let them be alive again,
let me not know them by name.
No prayer is big enough for some things.

FOR MARTIN LUTHER KING, JR.

After all the formal baptisms of water,
without ceremony
he entered the Jordan of his own blood.

We have been looking for gurus
to move quietly among us
and have not heard the thunder
of souls breaking out of bodies.

Life and death are on television,
dancing
in the words of followers and leaders,
electric and indistinct.
CBS and NBC cannot weep. In their pictures
even tears seem black and white.
No blood drips from the screen
onto my living room floor. Yet,
I walk around it. Lord,
I say to someone I have never seen,
Make me transparent.
Make us all transparent.

THE PUBLIC INTEREST
for Robert Kennedy

Somewhere in a politician
dead
by gunshot
is supposed to be a moral.
In the truckloads
becoming planeloads
of bodies coming home from war,
I look for a truckload of morals.

Honest men who speak
without dying
we treat like children
interrupting.
The dead men have the floor.
Tears dripping from their
mouths,
they try to seem
alive.

They have the ears of the poor
like ears of dead enemies
cut off,
afraid
to touch them.
If they could forget compassion
and wear
those ears —
the rattle
of small change,
the children crying for their
dead mother's soup.

POLITICO

No more cause to complain,
the lovable hero is here,
hearing complaints from anyone.
He is the defending champion.

He practices self-denial,
has become a celibate,
speaks kindly of the dying.
He answers every complaint

      after careful thought

promises relief
with a loving look.
People's faces show
he has spoken straight
into their hearts. I come closer
wanting to hear these promises
this first honest politician makes.
Over and over
he is repeating his name.

EACH AT ITS OWN TIME

Beginning with blowflies
five hundred kinds of kind insects
bury a dead buffalo,
each coming at its own time
above or below the body.
But the grasshopper
comes like a farmer
before the buffalo dies
to waste the grass
and starve the strong.

*IV. SOME GOOD THINGS LEFT AFTER THE WAR
WITH THE SIOUX*

WILLMAR AT NIGHT

I have been to Willmar, Minn.,
where the houses look pious.
At night they hear noises,
metal wheels squeaking and hissing,
the throb of engines biding their time.
The houses turn over in their sleep,
dreaming of following boxcars,
windows wide open, wind whupping
through parlors and bedrooms,
finally, in Fargo or St. Paul,
letting strangers enter
with whiskey and loud phonographs.
I have been to Willmar, slept in Willmar,
crossed the tracks in Willmar at night.

GRANDMOTHER

In her house I learned to listen to seashells.
The house full of the smells of raisin bread,
chicken soup, blackberry wine,
lavender sachet, laundry bluing, and coal smoke.
The smell of work.

Bronchial pneumonia is a dying old person's
best friend, according to the doctor.
106 degrees for three days,
but cold hands.
She seems to remember everyone all right,
but who knows what she knows,
who knows what she forgets?
"What do you think of an 80-year-old woman
having a baby?" she asks.
"I'm beautiful," she says.

It's finally her day off.

Her homemade rag rugs
lie on the gray linoleum,
the blank TV faces potted plants.
Her wedding portrait rests in the closet,
young and narrow-waisted, holding
blue carnations.

She comes forth like a flower.
And withers.
Blue carnations in her casket,
rosary in her hands:

her last wishes:

"I want my children to take
what they gave me.
I won't need it anymore.
Maybe I missed something

so forgive me."

She has stopped working.
She got sick picking up apples
on the hill behind the house
so they wouldn't rot.
The house is full of medicine
she will not need.
An electric clock buzzes.
The refrigerator hums.
I learned to listen to seashells here.

Her last confinement.
With the skill of a woman
who has done it a dozen times,
she bears down steadily,
gives birth to the spirit
she has carried full term.

Coming in from both coasts,
the family closes around her
like a flower closing for the night.
After the burial Friday morning
we open up,
enjoying each other's company
we have not had for so long,
and settle her estate in an hour or so,
and keep what we had given her,
and sing, and look
through old photographs.
And some who have been feuding
for years
sit down to dinner together.
And I listen to seashells in the attic.
She has not stopped working.
It seems as though we are
gathered around to see her new child.

ASTRONAUTS

In the hot middle of July,
climbing to the moon
on a beanstalk of fire,
they visit a giant of rock
and tell him their names
Maybe they see a golden egg
to bring back.

To step down and not hear the crunch of soil under your
feet, feel the foot lift, then go up as if seeking one more step
at the top of a staircase; to see the whole world you have just
stepped down from; to leap like a grasshopper away from
disapproving ants; to find you can dance six times better than
ever; to have ridden here in place of a bomb that could have
landed on earth, or might yet; to be the star attraction in the
center ring of an empty circus tent.

If I don't mind my sweat running
in this close air,
it is because the rocks
they brought back from the sky
are magic beans
I would gladly trade
for all the ice
in all the capitals of the earth.

THE TIME BEING
(after Paul Granlund's sculpture)

A man coming forward
leaves a hole in time
he cannot see any more
than the hole in space
where he just was.
He can pivot, flex,
bend, reach, spin,
chase himself in circles,
and never see it.
He leaves it all behind,
the print of the face,
the work of the hands,
the mark of the nerves,
like a trail of coins
dropped for someone else
to collect or spend.
He peels the past forward,
rips the future back.
He is a wedge in time.
He moves at angles
to everything,
splits time
into the geometry of dance.
His sweat
has the smell of forever.
Too much energy
to stay quiet
on any surface,
he reaches up, and out,
to eat the stars.
For him
the sun is gold,
the moon is silver,
the earth
is round
and worth saving.

SOME GOOD THINGS LEFT AFTER THE WAR
WITH THE SIOUX

My eyes welcome high grass,
green going yellow
shooting up
from old old earth
fed with hard-earned blood
and bled sweat.
This soil now marked by tractor tires
fed Amos Huggins in 1862
and feeds me now,
feeds you,
and the blood it has swallowed
never spoils the corn.
It is the magic of that blood,
red cells and white cells,
and clear yellow fluid
falling on the warm black earth,
that keeps legs pumping
up the valley and over the bluffs
to mourn the innocent,
to cherish the giving,
to pray with fast breath
to the breath of the land,
nitrogen rising
from remains of quiet and boastful alike,
seeping into the roots of rosebushes,
the strength of wheat,
the warmth of beans,
the sweetness of corn and pork,
the plumpness of lovers,

into children of grass and grain
and the spirit of the blood,
hundred-proof blood,
drunk-making blood,
man-making blood,
blood contaminated only by blood,
into the children of the eye,
of the spleen,
of the brain and the voice,
into the welcomers of grass,
welcomers of dawn
on the blue and brown earth,
welcomers of silence
and forgivers of fire and the plow and old murders.

UTOPIA

I dreamed of a perfect America,
and all the traffic lights
were green going out of every city
and red going in.

Books of Poetry from Three Rivers Press

Chapbooks

Uccello's Horse, Richard R. O'Keefe (1972)
The Dancer's Step, Ann Hayes (1973)
By Breathing In and Out, Albert Drake (1974)
The Obedience School, Greg Kuzma (1974)
Election, William L. Fox (1974)
Tonight is the Night of the Prom, Mark Jarman (1974)

Full Length Collections

Petroglyphs, Sam Hamill (1975)
The Lady From The Dark Green Hills, Jim Hall (1976)
An American Gallery, John Calvin Rezmerski (1977)